JOHN AND SEBASTIAN
CABOT

JOHN AND SEBASTIAN
CABOT

Henry Ira Kurtz

A Visual Biography

Illustrated with authentic prints and maps

Franklin Watts, Inc. / New York / 1973

For my mother and father

Historical Consultant,
Professor Richard Whittemore
Teachers College, Columbia University

Original maps and drawings by William Plummer
Cover design by Rafael Hernandez

Library of Congress Cataloging in Publication Data

Kurtz, Henry I
    John and Sebastian Cabot.

    (A Visual biography)
    SUMMARY: A biography of the Venetian ex-
plorer who laid the first English claim to the North
American continent and of his son, Sebastian, who
himself made several voyages of discovery.
    1. Cabot, John, d. 1498?–Juvenile literature. 2.
Cabot, Sebastian, 1474 (ca.)-1557–Juvenile litera-
ture. [1. Cabot, John, d. 1498? 2. Cabot, Sebastian,
1474 (ca.)-1557. 3. Explorers]
I. Title.
E129.C1K87   973.1'7'0922 [B] [920]   72-12796
ISBN 0-531-00970-X

Other Visual Biographies

Prince Henry the Navigator
Christopher Columbus

A Note on the Illustrations

Most of the illustrations in this book were drawn at the time of the Cabots. The beautiful drawings of Venice, in particular, give an idea of the power and wealth of Europe in the 1500's. There are two important maps of the period reproduced here, the Juan de la Cosa map that shows English flags along the coast of North America, and the map that Sebastian Cabot himself drew.

The original maps and drawings done for this book by William Plummer are indicated by the initials WKP.

Holiday festivities on a Venetian canal in the 1600s.

DARING VOYAGER

On August 23, 1497, an Italian merchant living in London sat down to write a letter to his brothers in Venice. He was excited about some news that had been reported a few days earlier. A fellow Italian had returned safely to England after making a daring voyage across the Atlantic Ocean. With obvious pride, the merchant wrote: "That Venetian of ours who went with a small ship from Bristol to find new lands has come back, and says that he has discovered mainland 700 leagues away, which is the country of the Great Khan [of China]. . . ." According to the letter writer, London was in an uproar. People cheered the explorer wherever he went. The king of England himself was "much pleased" with the results of the voyage. For if the reports were true, the explorer had found a direct sea-lane to the riches of Asia.

The center of all this attention was a former merchant and map-maker whose Italian name was Giovanni Caboto. In England he was known as John Cabot. Three months earlier he had set out to fulfill a long-held dream. Across the western seas, in the far-off lands of Asia, there were said to be golden-domed cities, jeweled palaces, and islands rich in spices and pearls. Like Christopher Columbus before him, Cabot hoped to reach those fabled oriental kingdoms by sailing west. And like Columbus, Cabot thought he had succeeded when he had actually failed. But it was a glorious failure. Cabot had not reached China as he believed. Instead he had stumbled across the continent of North America and had given England a claim to part of the New World.

Yet while Columbus, Magellan, and other explorers are famous figures of the past, few people have heard of John Cabot. After his death, his son Sebastian falsely claimed that he alone had made the North American discoveries. Until the truth became known in the late 1800s, John Cabot remained a forgotten man of history. Today he is still a shadowy figure who receives only passing mention in many history books.

A MAN OF THE RENAISSANCE

John Cabot lived during an era of history known as the Renaissance (a French word meaning "rebirth"). The Renaissance began in Italy during the fourteenth century and was marked by a revival of interest in learning and the arts. "The Renaissance was not a political or religious movement," one historian has written; "it was a state of mind." People took new interest in the writings of the ancient Greeks and Romans. Scholars also began their own studies in sciences such as geography. It was a time for trying new things. Renaissance philosophers spread the idea that a man with energy and a keen mind could do whatever his abilities would allow. Even someone of humble birth could perform great deeds.

It was against the background of the Renaissance that the Age of Exploration took place. Actually the Renaissance was a period of exploration and discovery in more ways than one. Everywhere people went out to explore the world and record their

An imaginative woodcut of the 1500s showing a monster believed to exist in the sea.

findings: the writer with his pen; the artist with his paint and brush; the navigator with his cross-staff and compass. John Cabot was a child of his times. Like other men of the Renaissance, he wanted to search beyond the known frontiers of the world. And so he became an oceangoing trailblazer — one of a small band of brave mariners who left the safe harbors of Europe to challenge the Western Ocean.

Besides being the home of many outstanding Renaissance artists and thinkers, Italy was the birthplace of two of the greatest explorers of that age: Christopher Columbus and John Cabot. In fact, the two men responsible for the European discovery of the American continents were born in the same city at about the same time. Columbus was born in Genoa around 1451. Cabot is believed to have been born there between 1450 and 1455. His year of birth is usually given as 1450.

3

Unfortunately, much less is known about Cabot than about Columbus. Historians have had to play detective to piece together tiny scraps of information about Cabot's early life. We do not even have a physical description of John or his notorious son Sebastian. This much we do know. John's father was a merchant named either Egidius or Julio Caboto. He had two sons, John (Giovanni) and Piero, and possibly other children as well. When John was about eleven years old, the Caboto family moved to Venice.

A document in the Venice Archives of State informs us that "a privilege of citizenship" was granted to John Cabot in March of 1476. At about the same time he married a Venetian woman named Mattea. They had three sons, whose names were Lewis, Sebastian, and Soncio. (Sebastian was probably born around 1480.) Not much more is known about John Cabot in those years, except that he was involved in the sale of real estate and in other business activities.

"THE QUEEN OF THE ADRIATIC"

Venice in John Cabot's time was at the peak of its power and splendor. The independent republic — sometimes called the "Queen of the Adriatic Sea" — ruled over a small empire. The city itself sparkled like a dazzling jewel. A French diplomat called

Venice "the most triumphant city that I have ever seen." Situated in a shallow lagoon at the northern edge of the Adriatic Sea, Venice sprawled over a hundred small islands. Connecting these islands was a crisscrossing network of canals and some four hundred bridges. The canals were the streets of the city. They were lined with shining palaces built by wealthy merchant families. Behind their marble walls were lovely gardens and courtyards filled with statues. Paintings by Renaissance masters decorated the spacious, richly furnished rooms inside the palaces.

Trade made this luxury possible. Venice grew rich from its commerce in Eastern spices, jewels, silks, and slaves. Money poured in from every corner of Europe and the East. The city was Europe's greatest transshipment port — a place where goods are received and then shipped to other points. Its crowded docks overflowed with goods from all parts of the civilized world — as it was then known to Europeans. Ships from northern Europe unloaded cloth and hides from England and Flanders, silver from central Europe, and steel from the German states. Venetian galleys carried these raw materials to Eastern ports. They returned with nutmeg and cinnamon from the Indies (or Southeast Asia); hand-woven rugs from Persia; perfumes from Arabia; silk and cotton fabrics from China and India.

Venice's great fleet was the pride of the republic. It was said to number over three thousand galleys — large ships that carried both sails and oars. Venetian ships were constructed in an enormous shipyard called the Arsenal, one of the wonders of the Renaissance world. The Arsenal was the largest manufacturing plant in Europe. Within its walls thousands of workmen built ships at an amazing rate. When the hull of a ship was finished, it was towed along a canal lined with warehouses and shops. From the windows of the building, workers passed out masts, oars, weapons, and supplies. By the time the ship had reached the end of this assembly line, it was fully equipped and ready to sail.

THE MERCHANT OF VENICE

As a Venetian and the son of a merchant, it is no surprise that Cabot decided to enter the field of trade. At that time the spice trade was the most rewarding business open to a Venetian trader. It offered

Venice, showing the Arsenal (right, center) and shipping. Two portions of a wood engraving by Jacopo de Barbari, 1500.

an opportunity for wealth as well as the adventure of travel to exotic Asian lands. For John Cabot the spice trade was the key that unlocked the door to the romantic East. Spices were then more important to the average European than all the jewels and silks of Cathay (the name given to China). They were used to preserve and flavor foods and to make drugs. Today we can put meat in a refrigerator or freezer and it will keep fresh for a fairly long time. But five hundred years ago the only way to preserve meat was to dry or salt it. As months went by, the meat became tougher and less appetizing. To make it edible, a housewife of the fifteenth century had to flavor it heavily with spices.

7

The source of the spices was a group of tropical islands off the southeastern coast of the Asian mainland. From these "Spice Islands" came the cloves, nutmegs, cinnamon, pepper, and ginger sought after by Europeans. The spices were transported by ship across the Indian Ocean and up the Red Sea to Arabia, or by camel caravan across the breadth of Asia. It took many months for the caravans to make their way over mountain ranges and across blazing deserts. The spices were passed from one town to another, as if in a relay race. At each way station, traders bought them and then resold them for a higher price.

Alexandria, Mecca, and Constantinople were the final stops on the caravan routes. As a representative of a Venetian firm, Cabot traveled to Alexandria, the chief port of Egypt. From there he went across the Isthmus of Suez and the Arabian desert to Mecca. In the teeming Arab bazaars of this city, Cabot saw spices and other precious European-bound goods unloaded from the backs of groaning camels. Curious about where these things came from, he questioned the camel drivers. The camel men could only tell him that other caravans from beyond the desert of Arabia brought the jewels and spices to their towns. They also said that those caravan drivers had told them that their goods had come from even more distant parts of Asia.

Cabot reasoned, as he later told an acquaintance, that "if the easterners declare to the southerners that these things come from places far away from them and so on from one to the other, always assuming that the earth is round, it follows as a matter of course that the last of all must take them in the north towards the west." By this Cabot meant that the source of the spices was a part of Asia to the north and west of Europe.

While working as a merchant, Cabot learned about navigation — steering a ship and directing its course. He also mastered the difficult art of map-making, which required an artist's skills and a knowledge of mathematics. Cabot taught himself geography by

Marco Polo.

reading many books on the subject and carefully studying all of the existing maps he could obtain. Soon his mind became a storehouse of information about the world as it was then known.

Unfortunately Cabot picked up many of the wrong ideas held by the scholars of that day. For example, fifteenth-century geographers believed that a single ocean — called Mare Oceanus, the Ocean Sea — separated Europe from Asia. They also thought the earth was smaller than it really is, so they cut in half the actual distance by sea between the two continents. They knew nothing about North and South America or the Pacific Ocean. Cabot believed, as they did, that the Atlantic Ocean was a broad highway leading to the wealthy kingdoms of Asia.

Geographers and navigators in Cabot's time were greatly influenced by *The Book of Marco Polo*, written by the famous Venetian traveler of the thirteenth century. (Marco Polo traveled around China and other parts of Asia between 1271 and 1295.)

Cabot apparently knew portions of the book by heart, especially the description of the island of Cipango. (This name referred to the country we now call Japan.) Marco wrote glowingly of the land and its people. He claimed it was so rich in gold, pearls, and precious stones "that no one can tell its wealth."

However, Marco Polo never visited Cipango. His information came from others who claimed to have been there. He not only overstated the wealth of the country, but he placed Cipango much closer to Europe and farther south than it really was. Of course, Cabot had no way of knowing this. We can only imagine his wide-eyed wonderment as he read about giant, rose-colored pearls and palaces dripping with gold.

On the basis of his readings in geography — as well as the information he picked up as a spice merchant — Cabot came up with what he thought was an original idea. If only the Ocean Sea separated Europe from Asia, the quickest route to the spices and jewels was west by sea and not east by land. The idea of a western voyage to Asia had already taken root among a small group of European geographers and navigators — including Christopher Columbus. But Cabot was unaware of these men when he first formed his plan. As far as he knew, the idea was exclusively his.

Timing is crucial to any new venture. A century earlier, when the Mediterranean trade routes to the East were open, there would have been no interest in his project. Besides, fourteenth-century ships were not made to withstand the rough seas and shifting winds of the Atlantic. But events in the fifteenth century played into Cabot's hands. One factor was the rise of the "new monarchies." In Spain, France, and England strong rulers forged national states out of rival principalities and kingdoms. The "new monarchs" had the power and wealth to sponsor voyages of exploration. Advances in shipbuilding were another factor in Cabot's favor. The sturdy caravels and carracks of the fifteenth century were built to stand buffeting ocean winds and waves.

What forced Europeans to look westward, however, was the rise of the Ottoman (Turkish) Empire. In 1453 the Turks captured Constantinople, which controlled the narrow waterway linking the Black Sea to the Mediterranean. They had already conquered the Middle Eastern lands and part of Europe. Now they were in a position to choke off the flow of Eastern goods to the Western countries. In return for not doing so, they demanded high payments from European traders. Prices for spices and silks soared in the cities of Europe.

Cabot realized that a direct sea route to eastern Asia would undercut the Turks and other middlemen. Having formed his plan, he looked around for a backer. Venice was out of the question. The Venetians had kept their monopoly of the spice trade by paying off the Turks. But there were other seafaring nations in Europe that might be interested. Portugal, Spain, and England were the best possibilities. Trade was important to these nations, and they had the necessary ships and seamen.

The evidence at hand indicates that Cabot went first to Spain and then to Portgual. According to fifteenth-century Spanish documents, a John Cabot Montecalunya lived in Valencia, a city on the east coast of Spain, in the early 1490s. In 1492 this Cabot drew up plans for improving the city's harbor. There is a striking similarity between John Cabot Montecalunya and the man who later appeared in England. Both men were Venetians who knew how to draw charts and diagrams, and both had an interest in seafaring. If this was the same Cabot, then he may have been among the crowd of well-wishers who turned out to greet Columbus when he returned in 1493 from his first voyage.

Unfortunately the Columbus voyage spoiled Cabot's chances for getting royal backing in Spain. His petition to Portugal's government was also turned down. The Portuguese were more interested in a sea route to the East Indies around the southern tip of Africa. But there was one other good possibility: England.

11

There were small colonies of English traders in the major ports of Spain and Portugal. From them Cabot could have learned that in recent years English ships from Bristol had been going out to explore the Atlantic. News about these voyages may have convinced him that he would find the support he needed in England. In any event, sometime before 1496 Cabot moved with his family to the British Isles.

BRISTOL, BRASIL, AND THE SEVEN CITIES

Once in England, Cabot settled in Bristol rather than London, where there was a large Italian business community. His choice was sound. Bristol was the most important English port facing the Atlantic, and so the logical starting point for a westward voyage of exploration. Bristol was a bustling, prosperous town at the junction of the river Avon and the river Frome — about eight miles inland from where the Avon empties into the Bristol Channel. Its narrow, cobblestone streets were lined with neat rows of brick-and-timber houses. Cabot rented a small house on Saint Nicholas Street for the sum of forty shillings a year. But even this small rental may have strained his purse, for he seems to have been in financial trouble at this point in his life. Observers described him as "a poor man" who earned a modest living by making maps and charts.

On the other hand, Cabot was also remembered as an intelligent man with a "keen wit." He had an agreeable personality and

Bristol in the 1600s, showing shipping on the rivers. A section of Millerd's plan of the city.

a certain magnetism that drew people to him. These attractive qualities enabled him to make friends among the Bristol merchants and shipowners. They included Robert Thorne and Hugh Elyot, two of the city's most prominent businessmen. Cabot discussed his plan for a western voyage with these men. They, in turn, provided details about the city's trading interests and its recent voyages of exploration.

At that time, Bristol was second only to London as a major English port. The city's merchants traded with Ireland, Spain, Portugal, and other countries in Europe. A profitable trade had also been built up with Iceland, to the north. Bristol ships carried salt and English woolen cloth to the Icelanders. They returned with barrels of codfish and other seafood. By the 1480s, however, the Iceland trade began to decline. The merchants and fishermen of Bristol went out to search for new fishing grounds and new markets for their cloth.

In those days, there was widespread belief in the existence of imaginary islands, which sailors — and some geographers — claimed were located in the Atlantic. One of these mythical islands was called Brasil and was said to lie off the western coast of Ireland. Another was known as the Island of the Seven Cities. Both were supposed to be fabulously wealthy. Beginning in 1480, Bristol ships went out into the Atlantic to search for these islands. From then on, the voyages continued on a regular basis.

The Bristol ships may have gone as far as the waters off present-day Canada. Anyway, some of the seamen talked of having seen the hazy outline of a distant land to the south and west of Greenland. The information excited Cabot. The land they had sighted might be one of the offshore islands of Asia — or even the mainland. If only he could get a ship and backing, he would sail

British ships of the 1400s in harbor and approaching the coast. A drawing from the Hastings Manuscript, about 1480.

to the new lands, pick up the coast, and cruise south. From his knowledge of geography, he reasoned that if the coastline followed a southwesterly direction, it would definitely be Asia.

Things now seemed to be working in Cabot's favor. The Bristol men had marked a path across the ocean that he could follow. There were experienced seamen in Bristol who knew these waters, and some of them might be talked into a signing on for his venture. The prize was certainly big enough. If Bristol could divert the spice trade to its docks, it would become the richest port in Europe. The local merchants liked the idea and quickly fell in with his plan. They agreed to supply money and ships if Cabot could get the king's approval. With their help, Cabot arranged to go to London to present his case. Fortunately for him, England was then ruled by King Henry VII, a shrewd monarch who had a businessman's love of profits.

THE NOT-SO-MERRY ENGLAND OF KING HENRY VII

In 1485 Henry Tudor, a nobleman of the house of Lancaster, defeated the Yorkist King Richard III at the Battle of Bosworth Field. A few months later, the victor was crowned King Henry VII of England. So began the Tudor dynasty, which lasted until the death of Queen Elizabeth I in 1603.

The England taken over by Henry VII was a nation in shambles. Plague and wars — including a long civil war — had left the country economically ruined and politically divided. Trade

16

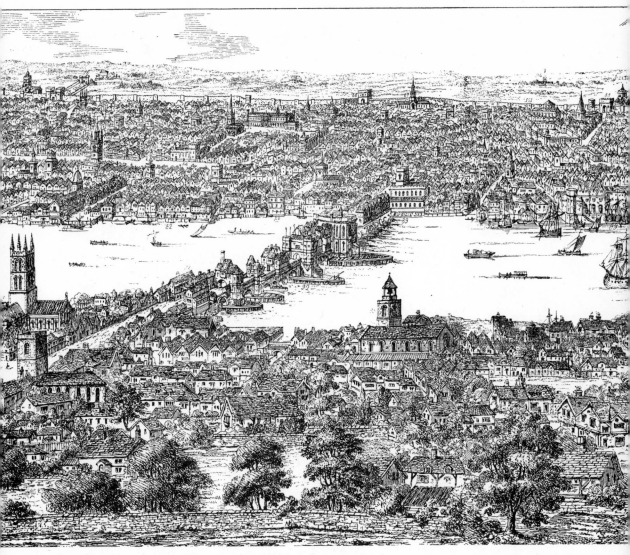

London in the 1500s.

was in decline, and the royal treasury was nearly empty. Henry's task was to build a strong nation-state out of the ruins of his shattered kingdom. The new king set about to restore law and order in England. He also began to build up his treasury. Henry found many ways to bring in money, including increased local taxes and high customs duties on foreign goods. Previous kings had usually imprisoned or beheaded lawless nobles. Henry often chose instead to make them pay heavy fines. In this way, he filled the royal

17

coffers and earned a reputation as a merciful king. Under Henry's rule, England prospered and became more stable. For the most part, the king avoided costly overseas wars and maintained good relations with foreign powers. He encouraged trade, enlarged the merchant fleet, and built up the wool and cloth industries at home.

Henry's frugal policies helped to create this new prosperity. But although the king was thrifty, he was no miser. He liked pomp and ceremony, and he enjoyed wearing expensive robes and jewels. The English court was noted for its colorful tournaments and lavish feasts. Sometimes as many as seven hundred nobles dined at the king's expense in the royal banquet hall at the Tower of London.

"TO OUR WELL-BELOVED JOHN CABOT..."

It was to the court of this wary and calculating monarch that John Cabot came one day, in 1495, to plead his case. No record exists of Cabot's interview with the king, but such a meeting surely took place. King Henry was his own first minister. He would not have put the royal stamp on such an unusual matter without looking over the man who proposed it. From what we know to have followed, we can assume that Cabot was very persuasive.

His first point would have been that Columbus had not reached Asia, merely some outlying islands. Therefore, the English could still beat the Portuguese and Spaniards to Cathay and Cipango. Cabot would have argued also that Asia was closer to En-

King Henry VII of England.

gland than to its seafaring rivals. The reason for this is that the earth is a sphere and the distance around it is shorter in the northern latitudes and greater in the south. Since Bristol ships had already explored the Atlantic Ocean past Greenland, his voyage would merely be the final step on the road to Asia. Success would give England a monopoly of the spice trade and undreamed-of wealth.

King Henry was open to the idea. He was well informed about the Bristol voyages and those of the Spanish and Portuguese navigators. In fact, he had turned down an opportunity to sponsor Christopher Columbus's first voyage. Henry was not going to make the same mistake twice. Besides, he did not have to put up money or provide ships; both would come from the Bristol merchants. All that Cabot wanted was the king's seal of approval to back up his claim to any new lands he found.

But there were some risks involved on Henry's part. Above all, there was the possibility of conflict with Spain and Portugal. Both of these countries had staked out claims in the Atlantic. To avoid a clash, they had signed the Treaty of Tordesillas in June, 1494. Under the terms of the treaty, an imaginary line was drawn from the North Pole to the South Pole 370 leagues (about 1,100 miles) west of the Cape Verde Islands. Spain was granted all lands west of the line, while Portugal got those to the east.

King Henry had not signed the treaty, however, and was not legally bound by it. He therefore made a bold decision. He would respect the claims of Spain and Portugal to all undiscovered lands in the southern latitudes. But he would allow Cabot to explore the western seas in the same latitude as England. It was a calculated risk, but one worth taking in view of the stakes. Besides, the English monarch knew that Spain was anxious to keep England as a friendly ally in case of war with France. Henry felt sure that Ferdinand and Isabella, the Spanish rulers, would not react too strongly to the Cabot project.

After due consideration, the king issued a charter (letters patent) addressed to "our well-beloved John Cabot." According to the Letters Patent of March 5, 1496, Cabot and his sons were given "full and free authority . . . to sail to all parts, regions, and coasts of the eastern, western, and northern sea." On behalf of the king they had the right "to find, discover, and investigate" any new lands "which before this time were unknown to Christians." Simply put, Henry was saying that any land not already claimed by a Christian power (such as Spain) belonged to whoever got there first.

Cabot and his heirs were given permission to take joint possession of, and occupy, in the king's name, any lands they found, "however numerous they may be." In return for his generosity, the king expected to receive "either in goods or money" one-fifth of all the profits that resulted from the discoveries they made.

OUT FROM BRISTOL

Cabot was naturally eager to get started. A short time after the letters patent were issued, he sailed out of Bristol with a single ship. But the first attempt ended in failure. It was an unfortunate set-back, which might have caused a lesser man to give up. But although he was surely disappointed, Cabot was far from defeated. He had overcome too many obstacles to be stopped now. During the next months Cabot made more careful arrangements for a second attempt. The evidence suggests that he was allowed to build his own ship.

The new ship was a three-masted cog (a small sailing vessel) of fifty tons. Tonnage in those days meant something completely different from what it does today. Ships then were measured in terms of the number of tuns — wine casks — that could be stored below deck. Normally, about fifty to a hundred of these casks could be carried, depending on the size of the ship. Cabot's vessel was about sixty or seventy feet long — no bigger than a large yacht. There is an interesting possibility that the ship was originally named *Mattea*, in honor of Cabot's wife, but that the English sailors called her the *Matthew* in their own language.

After months of preparation, Cabot was ready to sail again. One day toward the end of May, 1497, the *Matthew* cast off from Bristol's docks and glided down the Avon River to the open sea. On board were eighteen men besides Cabot. Little is known about the crew except that it included a French sailor from Burgundy and an Italian barber, and that most of the others were English.

til ye come in to iiij. fadun deep and yf it be stremy
grounde it is betwene shifestatt and tille in the entre
of the chanel of fflaundres and soo goo yowre cours
til ye have xvti fadun deep. than goo est northe est
a longe the see. + c

Robert Thorne and Hugh Elyot, Cabot's merchant friends, may have accompanied him. His son Sebastian, who was then in his teens, may have gone along. But he was certainly not in a position of leadership as he later claimed.

And so, on that fateful May morning, Cabot "committed himself to fortune," as an acquaintance later remarked. This was to be only a scouting mission. Cabot was hoping to reach the Asian mainland. But he would settle for some offshore islands that could be used as a base for future trading voyages.

The *Matthew* sailed around the southern coast of Ireland before heading out into the Atlantic. For the most part, the seas remained calm during the outward voyage. But in the squat, shallow-draft ships of the fifteenth century even a gentle swell would have seemed rough to us. Shaped like oversized bathtubs, these vessels pitched and rolled with every movement of the sea. In a storm they were tossed about like rowboats.

On board the *Matthew*, as on other ships of the time, sailors had to put up with many hardships. Sleeping quarters and kitchen facilities were not provided for the crew. The ordinary seaman slept wherever he could find a fairly warm and dry place. Most preferred to sleep on deck, where the air was cleaner. The lower decks were usually wet, stinking, and crawling with rats and roaches. Water constantly leaked through the flimsy planking, and the wooden pumps had to be manned around the clock to prevent the ship from being flooded.

Cabot and his crew were surely wet and miserable throughout the voyage. The food they ate could only have made them feel worse. Salted beef and pork, along with hard biscuits and dried peas, made up the daily menu. After weeks at sea, the meat became wormy, and the biscuits stale and grimy with salt water

An English ship of the 1400s, a drawing from the Hastings Manuscript, about 1480.

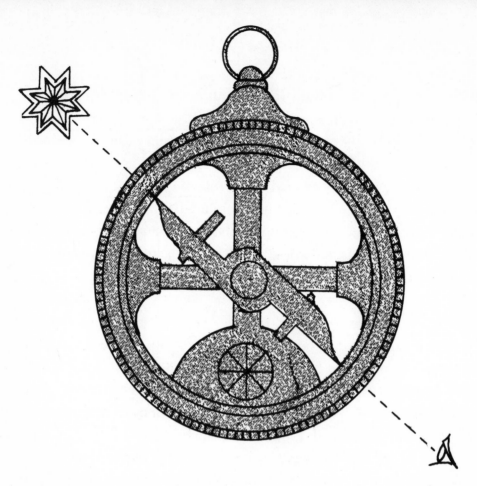

MARINERS' ASTROLABE

and ship's dirt. Drinking water was kept in large open barrels on deck. The exposed water easily became contaminated and often caused serious illness.

Although the winds were with him most of the way, Cabot still had his problems navigating a course. Various instruments were available to help him fix his position at sea. Among them were the astrolabe and the cross-staff, which were used to determine latitude — the distance north or south of the equator measured in degrees. Both had to be aimed at the sun or a star. Once the sight was fixed, a reading could be taken from a scale of degrees.

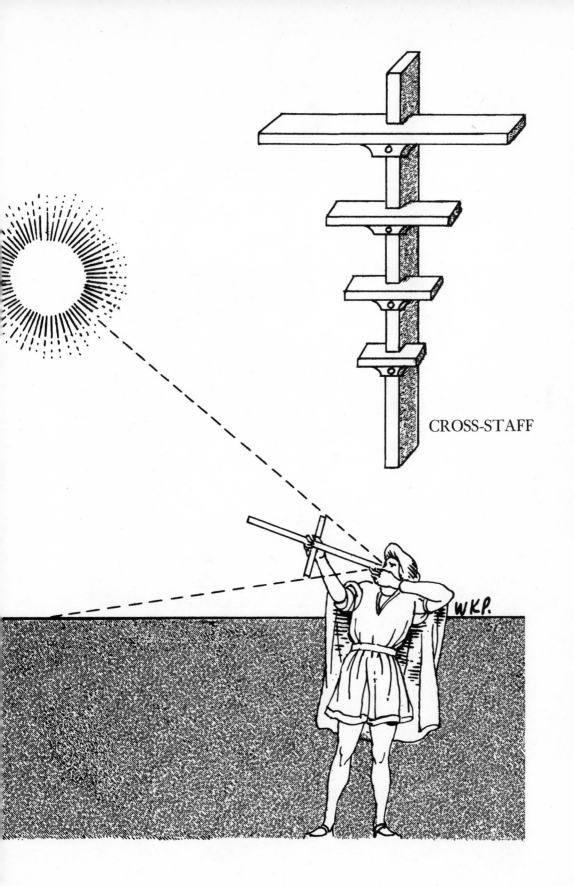

CROSS-STAFF

A Spanish astrolabe in brass, with a star map of Islamic design.

But it was not easy to line up these instruments properly on a pitching and rolling ship. More often than not, the readings were way off. Like many of his fellow navigators, Cabot favored a method called dead reckoning to determine his position. Dead reckoning is a simple technique. The navigator sets his course by his compass and then keeps track of the number of miles he sails during a given period of time. Thus he always has a fair idea of where he is in relation to the point from which he started.

Dead reckoning has its own problems, however. In order for it to work properly, an accurate device for measuring speed and a good ship's clock are necessary. Neither was available in the fifteenth century. Speed was measured by throwing a wood chip into the water from the bow of the ship and estimating how long it took for it to reach the stern. However, a ship might run into a head wind, which required tacking — sailing in a zigzag pattern. This was likely to throw off a navigator's calculations.

In spite of these problems, Cabot managed to keep the *Matthew* on a fairly stable course. But the going was slow, owing to contrary winds and the eastward flow of the Gulf Stream. It took more than thirty days to reach the area where they hoped to discover Asia. A few days before sighting land, the little ship ran into a storm and was knocked about. Fortunately no serious damage was done.

The coast of Newfoundland, one of the possible landing places of John Cabot.

THE NEW FOUND LAND

By this time, Cabot and his men could see signs of land. An occasional broken tree branch and some leaves and twigs floated by them in the water. At about 5 A.M. on the morning of June 24, 1497 — Saint John the Baptist's Day — a crewman looked through the morning haze and saw the dim outline of land on the horizon. Cabot decided to call it simply *Prima Terra Vista* — first-seen land. The *Matthew* dropped anchor close to the forested shoreline, and Cabot ordered a boat put out. Accompanied by a small party of men, he went ashore.

Historians continue to argue about the exact site of Cabot's landing. Some scholars claim it was made on the coast of Labrador or Newfoundland. Others believe it was probably Nova Scotia or Cape Breton Island. (All of these points are in present-day Canada.) Wherever Cabot landed on that historic morning, he and his men became the first Europeans known to have reached the North American mainland since Leif Ericson and his Vikings arrived there five hundred years earlier. After coming ashore, Cabot held a short ceremony in which he took possession of the new land in the name of the king of England. He planted a wooden cross and unfurled two flags — one bearing the Cross of Saint George of England and the other the lion of Saint Mark of Venice.

The day was mild, and they were in the midst of a great forest. It was later reported that "they found tall trees of the kind masts are made, and smaller trees, and the country is very rich in grass." Not far from shore, the explorers spotted a trail that led

SYMBOL OF ST. MARK

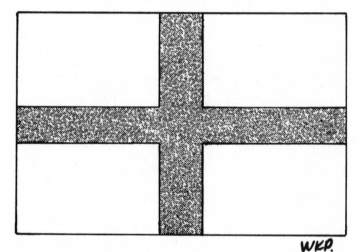

WKP.

CROSS OF ST. GEORGE

inland. Cabot and his men followed the trail for a short distance. No inhabitants were seen, but a campsite was discovered "where a fire had been made." Here the landing party found traces of farm animals and a painted stick about two feet long. They also picked up some traps for catching game and a needle of the type used to make fishing nets.

Cabot decided to be cautious, since there were obviously people living in the surrounding area. He had no way of knowing

30

if the inhabitants would be friendly or hostile. Perhaps at that very moment unfriendly eyes were peering at them from hiding places in the woods. Fearing an ambush, Cabot decided not to remain too long. He had his men fill their water casks, and then they returned quickly to the ship.

During the remaining days of June and throughout most of July, Cabot cruised along the coast of the newly discovered land. He sailed far enough to satisfy himself that it was part of a continent and not just an island. Although he continued his exploration for nearly a month, neither he nor any of his men went ashore again. By sailing close to land, however, they were able to see what looked like fields on the outskirts of villages. At one point, two figures were observed running through the trees. Were they humans or animals? They were too far away to be clearly seen.

But it was in the sea itself that the explorers made their most important discovery. All along the coast of this "new founde lande" the waters teemed with cod, haddock, and other fish. Cabot's men were able to catch them by the netful and by using baskets weighted with stones. Here were the fishing banks the Bristol men had been searching for.

Eventually Cabot worked his way back to Cape Race, the easternmost point of Newfoundland. He was convinced that he had reached the northeastern corner of the Asian mainland. His mission was a success, as he saw it. Therefore he was anxious to return to report his findings. Besides, his provisions were beginning to run low. Around July 20 Cabot took leave of the new lands and started back to Bristol.

The voyage home took only fifteen days, quite short for that time. Cabot had a favorable wind at his back and calm seas all the way home. On August 6, eleven weeks after he had left Bristol, Cabot returned in triumph. His Bristol backers were overjoyed when they learned of his discoveries. With several members of his crew, Cabot rode to London to make his report to the king.

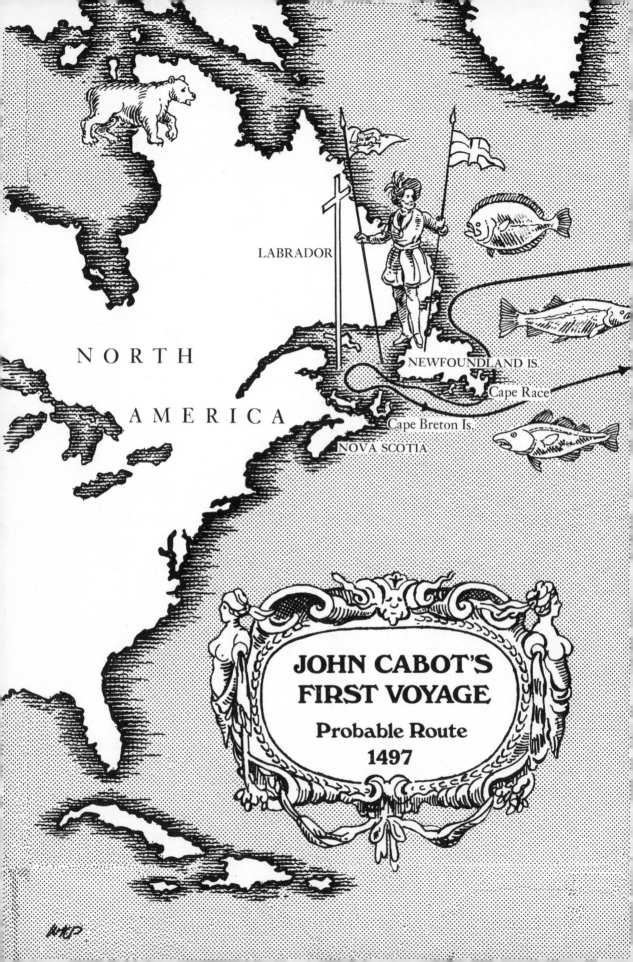

NORTH

AMERICA

LABRADOR

NEWFOUNDLAND IS.

Cape Race

Cape Breton Is.

NOVA SCOTIA

**JOHN CABOT'S
FIRST VOYAGE**

**Probable Route
1497**

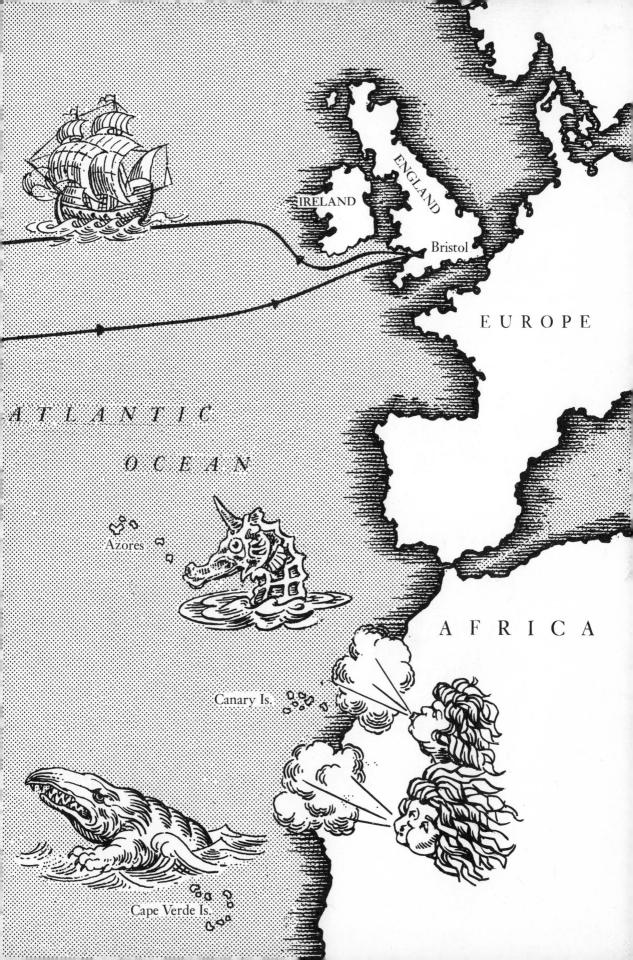

John Cabot, an imaginative representation on a commemorative medal.

"HE IS CALLED
THE GREAT ADMIRAL"

When the group arrived at the royal court, King Henry granted them an immediate audience. Cabot stated that he had reached Asia, and that his route was shorter than the one used by Columbus. He gave the king a colorful account of the voyage, using a globe and map of his own making. The traps and needle they had picked up were displayed as evidence, and Cabot described the land and the fisheries along the coast.

Such boasting was greeted with some doubt by the king, especially since the claims were made by a poor foreigner. But then the Bristol men spoke up and confirmed the story. Once convinced that Cabot had not exaggerated his findings, the king expressed great delight. He promised the discoverer more ships and men for another voyage the following spring. In the meantime, he gave him money to "amuse himself." True to form, however, Henry did not open his purse too wide. The explorer received a cash reward of ten pounds sterling. Later, a yearly pension of twenty pounds was added.

Word of Cabot's voyage spread quickly through London. Rumors flew from one end of the city to the other. Cabot has reached Cathay! He has discovered the Seven Cities! A dispatch was sent to the ruler of a southern European state informing him that "his Majesty here has gained a part of Asia, without the stroke of a sword." A Venetian merchant named Lorenzo Pasqualigo wrote proudly of the fact that Cabot had planted the banner of

Saint Mark of Venice in the new land "so that our flag has been hoisted very far afield."

Cabot was no longer an unknown map-maker; he had become a celebrity. "He is called the Great Admiral," one observer recorded, "and vast honor is paid to him and he goes dressed in silk, and these English run after him like mad." For the next few days, Cabot swaggered about the city, clearly enjoying his sudden fame and new prosperity.

Success has a way of going to a person's head, and Cabot was no exception. "My lord the Admiral esteems himself at least a prince," stated one who knew him. As befits a prince, Cabot generously granted titles and lands to members of his crew. He gave his Genoese barber an island all his own and awarded another to a French sailor who had been on the voyage. He also promised the title of bishop to several Italian friars if they would go along on his next voyage.

During the months that followed, Cabot worked hard planning another ocean crossing. He continued to live in Bristol, but he made occasional trips to London to confer with the king. On February 3, 1498, Cabot was granted new letters patent authorizing him to return to "the land and isles found by the said John in our name and by our commandment." This voyage was to be a more ambitious project than the first. After returning to the new lands, Cabot intended to cruise south until he reached Cipango and the Spice Islands. Along the way he would establish a trading colony to use as a jumping-off point for future voyages.

Not everyone was pleased about Cabot's plan. The Spanish ambassador to England protested to Henry that the lands discovered by Cabot belonged to Spain under the terms of the Treaty of Tordesillas. But the English king rejected the protest. Henry had a nose for profit, and he believed that the forthcoming voyage would result in greath wealth. He was not going to let the Spaniards discourage him from following up on Cabot's discoveries.

THE PERILOUS SEA

Five ships were outfitted for Cabot in the spring of 1498. Only one was provided by the king, who was still hesitant about dipping into the royal treasury. The other four ships were supplied by a group of London and Bristol merchants. Trading goods were stocked on board, including "coarse cloth, caps, laces, points, and other trifles." Cabot wanted to be ready to do business when he sailed into the great ports of Cipango and Cathay.

Early in May, 1498, Cabot's expedition set sail from Bristol. He was truly an admiral on this voyage — the captain general of a small fleet. Unfortunately, his glory was short lived. From the very outset, the voyage was ill-fated. A few days after leaving port, the flotilla ran into rough seas. Gale-force winds lashed the vessels and badly battered one of them. The damaged ship had to seek refuge in an Irish port.

Mystery surrounds the voyage after this unhappy beginning. However, it is almost certain that Cabot first sailed back to the waters off Newfoundland. From there he probably picked up the coast and headed south. Shortly after arriving in Newfoundland waters, the ships apparently became separated in a storm. Several of the vessels may have been lost at sea. The others continued on in an effort to locate Cipango and the Spice Islands. But only endless stretches of barren wilderness and occasional Indian villages awaited them.

Just how far south Cabot's ships traveled is anyone's guess. Some experts think he may have reached the mouth of the Chesa-

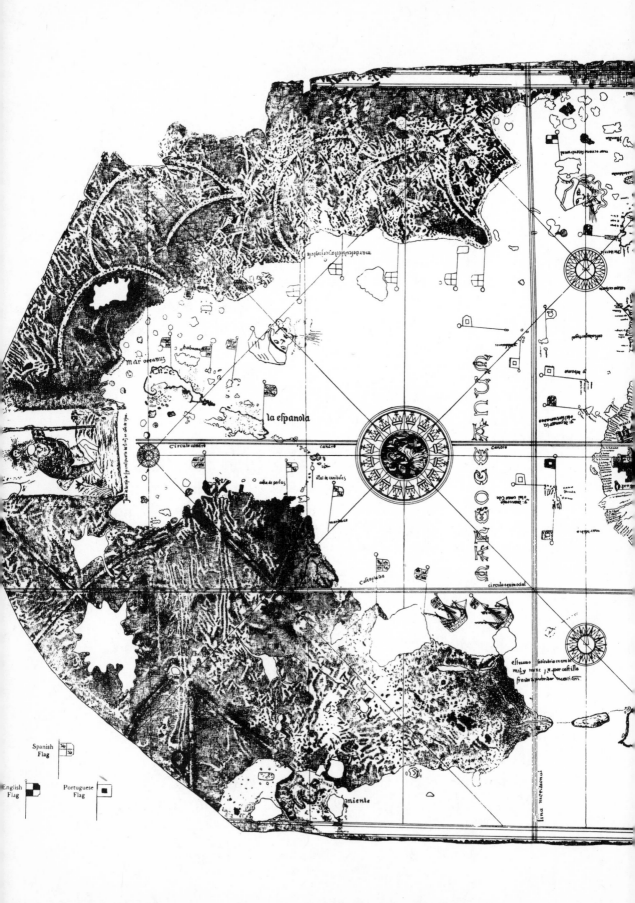

Spanish
Flag

English
Flag

Portuguese
Flag

mar oceanus

la efpanola

Circulo cancro

cancro

cancro

Circulo equinocial

mar del nucuo occidente

iflas de canibales

coſta de perlas

marañon

Cariapaña

Poniente

linia meridional

peake Bay, off the coast of Virginia. Others believe that at least one of his ships got as far as the Caribbean Sea. There are several interesting clues. In 1500 a Spanish navigator and map-maker named Juan de la Cosa — who had previously sailed with Columbus — drew a map showing the lands of the New World. La Cosa painted English flags along much of the coast of North America. These flags could very well mark the route of Cabot's second voyage.

Another clue came from the records concerning a Spanish explorer named Alonzo de Hojeda. In 1499 Hojeda went on a voyage of discovery to South America and the seas to the north. While in the area of the Bahama Islands, he apparently ran into an English ship. For in 1501 Hojeda was told to return to the area "where the English are making discoveries . . . so that you may stop the exploration of the English in that direction." The only English who could have been exploring there during that period were Cabot and his men. It is therefore likely that Hojeda met Cabot himself, or one of his ships, somewhere in the vicinity of the Caribbean Sea.

Some historians believe that survivors of Cabot's expedition returned to Bristol in 1499; others conclude that all were lost. Formerly it was thought that Cabot was among the possible survivors, and that he died in England about a year after his return. But in 1939 scholars found a manuscript of a sixteenth-century history of England, written by an Italian priest named Polydore Vergil. His book included a short account of Cabot's second voyage. According to Vergil, Cabot was lost at sea, "since after that voyage he was never again seen anywhere."

The New World on a map of the world drawn by Juan de la Cosa in 1500. The English flags seen along the coast of North America are considered evidence of John Cabot's second voyage.

Where and when Cabot went down may never be known. But it now seems certain that he died during the voyage. If Cabot did get as far as the Caribbean, he must have realized that he was on a fool's errand. The New Found Land was not Asia, but some strange wasteland with only a few poor and uncivilized people. This discovery would have been a bitter blow to Cabot. Perhaps it is best to believe that he went to his death in the full fury of a storm, still convinced that one day soon he would see the sun's golden rays glancing off the fabled palaces of Cipango.

THE LEGACY OF JOHN CABOT

After the voyage of 1498 British exploration of the New World came to a temporary halt. Both the king and the merchants who had paid for Cabot's second voyage were disappointed with the results. From a trader's point of view, the expedition had been a total loss. No jewels, silks, or spices had been brought back. Besides, Spanish protests against the English invasion of the new lands had become stronger. And King Henry did not want to weaken the bonds of friendship he had developed between himself and the Spanish monarchs.

Furthermore, it began to dawn on some people that the newly discovered lands were not a part of Asia. They must, therefore, be an unknown landmass—a New World. The Spaniards were the lucky ones, reasoned the English. They had discovered the part of the New World rich in gold and silver. All that Cabot had found

was a bleak woodland. Then, in 1499, word reached England that the Portuguese explorer Vasco da Gama had rounded Africa and reached India by sea. Da Gama returned to Portugal with cargoes of cinnamon, nutmeg, cloves, and other spices. The Venetian monopoly of the spice trade was broken. Within a short time, spices were being sold in Lisbon for a fraction of the price charged by the Venetians. King Henry and the English merchants could only shrug off their own failure.

But the Cabot voyages did produce one source of profit: the cod fisheries off Newfoundland and Nova Scotia. Fleets of English fishing vessels soon swarmed into these waters. The great catches of fish brought back each year on English ships more than repaid the Bristol merchants for their investment in Cabot's enterprise.

In the long run, however, there was a more important result of the voyages. They gave England a claim to a portion of North America, and they were the legal cornerstone of the English colonies that took root more than a century later. Who knows what course American history might have taken if John Cabot had not raised England's flag over the rugged coast of what is now Canada?

HISTORY'S FORGOTTEN MAN

In spite of his accomplishments, John Cabot quickly fell back into obscurity. No general history of the voyages was written in his time, and no logbook or other eyewitness account survived. The name John Cabot soon slipped from the public's mind. But it was not just forgetfulness that caused his memory to fade away. It was also due to the dishonesty of his son Sebastian. For his own selfish purposes, Sebastian claimed that he, and not his father, had been the leader of both voyages. By the mid-1500s Sebastian's place in the history books was secure, while his father lay unremembered and unmourned at the bottom of the ocean. Sebastian did nothing to correct the record. He was quite happy to have all the glory and fame for himself. Not even his closest friends learned the truth. He carried his secret to the grave.

Three centuries were to pass before the real story became known. During that time historians gave Sebastian full credit for the voyages made by his father. But in the 1800s scholars uncovered documents that revealed the true facts. Only then did John Cabot finally receive the recognition he deserves.

SEBASTIAN CABOT

History is full of colorful rogues and con men. Sebastian Cabot could have matched wits with the best of them. When it came to playing both ends against the middle without getting caught, he had few equals. Actually Sebastian seems to have been something of a split personality — like Dr. Jekyll and Mr. Hyde. On the one hand, he was a liar and fraud who posed as the man who discovered North America. On the other hand, he made his own mark as an explorer, navigator, map-maker, and business promoter.

Giambattista Ramusio, an Italian geographer of the sixteenth century, called him "a man of great and rare experience in the art of navigation and the science of cosmography [describing and mapping the world]." Modern historians are divided in their opinion of him. A few have branded Sebastian an outright scoundrel of whom little good can be said. Others claim that his accomplishments balance out his misdeeds. All of them agree that he was a clever person who took advantage of any opportunity to advance himself.

Following in his father's footsteps, Sebastian began his varied career as a map-maker. His profession provided him with a decent living, but it did not satisfy his appetite for wealth and high position. Ambition drove him into the field of exploration. Sebastian had learned a great deal about navigation and seamanship from his father, and he decided to put his knowledge to good use. The lure of Eastern wealth was as strong as ever in the early 1500s. Unfortunately, the western sea route appeared to be blocked by the new lands discovered by Cabot and Columbus. However, Sebastian believed that there might be a way around or through these continents — a Northwest Passage to Asia.

Sebastian took his idea to Henry VII, who had watched enviously as the Portuguese reaped great profits from their African route. The English king agreed that it was worth a try. Either in the spring of 1508 or the early months of 1509 Sebastian set out with two caravels. (Some historians question whether this voyage ever took place, claiming it was just another of Sebastian's tall tales; but the evidence seems to bear out the story that it did occur.)

The two ships sailed north to Greenland and up into the waters of Davis Strait. They arrived there in the summer "when the days were very long and almost without night, and the nights very clear." But as an account of the voyage written in 1516 notes, "even in the month of July he [Sebastian] found great icebergs floating in the sea." Along the way, they saw large bears, which plunged into the water to scoop up fish with their claws. Bitter-cold weather and ice floes forced them to turn west. Cruising along the Canadian coast, they discovered a waterway leading inland. Sebastian's ships sailed through the inlet and came to a large body of water.

Sebastian was overjoyed. He was sure they had found a passage to Cathay and that the vast sea before them was another ocean. Actually, they had sailed through what we now know as Hudson Strait and had entered Hudson Bay. By this time the cold and discomfort of the voyage had become too much for the crew. They became rebellious and demanded that Sebastian turn back. Faced with the threat of a mutiny, Sebastian retraced his steps and headed south to warmer waters. He hoped he would find another passage in a more comfortable climate. But after reaching a point near Cape Hatteras, North Carolina, the ship turned east and headed for England.

Back in Bristol, Sebastian learned that Henry VII had died and that his son, Henry VIII, was on the throne. Young Henry had no interest in voyages of exploration. He was more concerned with matters at home and with such youthful activities as sports and women. Sebastian decided to keep the secret of the passage to Asia to himself until he could get backing for another voyage. A few years later, in 1512, he traveled to Spain with an English army sent to help in a war against the French. While there, he transferred to the Spanish naval service.

WHEELING AND DEALING

For the next five years Sebastian was kept busy making maps for the Spanish navy. During that period he married a Spanish woman named Catalina de Medrano. Soon afterward he became a naval aide to King Ferdinand. Sebastian took advantage of the situation and tried to promote another voyage to the northwest. But in 1516 King Ferdinand died, and the project fell through.

In 1517 Sebastian went on leave to England. There he tried to get ships and men so that he could go back to the northwest waters. When this effort failed, he returned to Spain. Charles I (Charles V of the Holy Roman Empire) was now king. The new monarch thought highly of Sebastian and appointed him pilot major (chief navigator) of Spain. As an expert in geography and navigation, Sebastian supervised voyages of exploration and recorded new discoveries on the maps.

King Charles 1 of Spain (Charles V of the Holy Roman Empire).

But even this high-paying and important position was not enough for him. In 1520 he entered into secret negotiations with the English government. Once again he hoped to get backing for a northwest voyage to Asia. This was outright treachery on Sebastian's part, since it competed with a similar Spanish project. At that time, Ferdinand Magellan was sailing around South America on his way to Asia. His voyage (1519–22) opened up a direct sea route from Spain to the Spice Islands.

47

NORTH
AMERICA

SOUTH
AMERICA

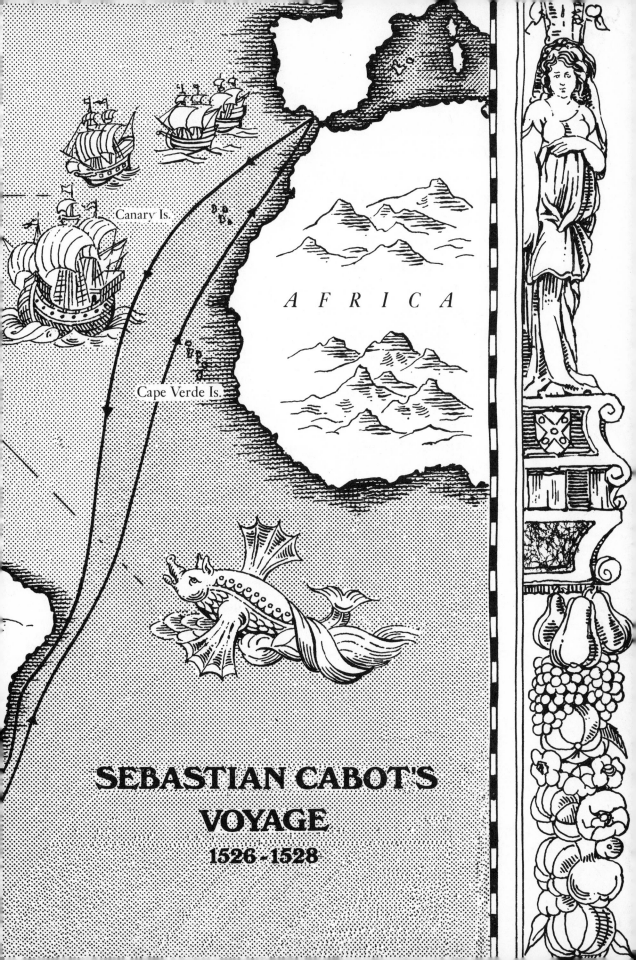

Canary Is.

Cape Verde Is.

AFRICA

SEBASTIAN CABOT'S
VOYAGE
1526-1528

As it turned out, the unscrupulous Sebastian fared no better this time than before. Back he went to Spain, a discouraged man. Shortly after returning, he learned that the Venetian government knew about his English activities and his claim to have found a passage to Asia. The news stunned him. If the Venetians informed the Spanish government about his double-dealing, he might be hanged for treason. But, as always, Sebastian was as slippery as an eel. He wriggled out of this difficult spot by promising to go to Venice and reveal his secret passage.

Sebastian never kept this promise, and four years later Spain sent him off on a voyage to South America. His orders were to follow Magellan's route to the Spice Islands of the East Indies. With four ships, he set sail from Spain on April 3, 1526. The expedition never reached the Pacific. Instead, the fleet worked its way down the coast of South America to the area of present-day Argentina. There friendly Indians told him about gold and silver deposits farther inland. Spurred on by these reports, Sebastian headed up the Rio de la Plata — River of Silver — named by its Spanish discoverer Juan Diaz de Solís in 1516.

The expedition was a total disaster. One of his ships ran aground and sank. There were skirmishes with the Indians, and in one ambush Sebastian lost more than twenty men. Arguments broke out between Sebastian and his officers, and a mutiny followed. Sebastian struck back by hanging some of the mutineers and putting others ashore in the jungle with only a few weapons and some food.

Sebastian sent back to Spain for reinforcements, claiming that he had found a land rich in gold and silver. Actually, the few silver objects he had found among the Indians came from much farther away — the Inca Empire in Peru. Supplies and more men were supposed to have been sent to him, but none arrived.

After four wasted years, Sebastian and his few remaining men returned home. A group of his officers immediately brought

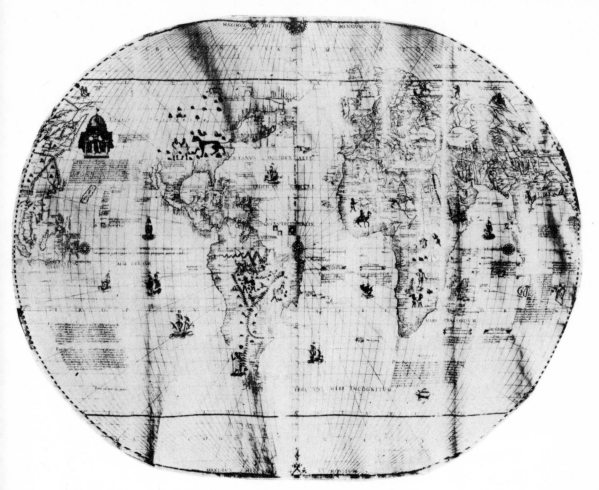

A map of the world drawn by Sebastian Cabot, published in 1544.

charges against him for abusing his men and disobeying his instructions for the voyage. Sebastian was tried and found guilty of these offenses. The court sentenced him to three years of exile in Morocco. But then King Charles stepped in on his behalf. The court's ruling was set aside and Sebastian was reinstated as pilot major.

Sebastian's life quieted down after that. He spent the next years carrying out his duties as pilot major and working on a new map of the world. The map was published in 1544 and included the North American discoveries of his father, his own South American explorations, and all of the Spanish and Portuguese discoveries up to that time. It quickly became a model followed by other map-makers.

IN SEARCH OF
THE NORTHWEST PASSAGE

Always the opportunist, Sebastian continued to maintain contact with the English government. In 1547 he was offered a post in England by King Edward VI, who had succeeded Henry VIII. Sebastian accepted and in January, 1548, returned to Bristol. He was placed in charge of England's maritime affairs and given a generous salary. The next few years were the highlight of Sebastian's career. He directed England's maritime life with skill and arranged favorable trade agreements with other European countries.

Sebastian and the English merchants were still looking for that elusive shortcut to Asia, however. In the early 1550s the Company of Merchant Adventurers was formed, and Sebastian was made its governor for life. The company's major purpose was to find a northern sea route to Cathay. After much discussion, it was decided to look for a Northeast Passage around Norway.

Sebastian was then too old to take part in the voyage himself, but he was the chief planner. Three ships were equipped and placed under the command of Sir Hugh Willoughby. Richard Chancellor, another able seaman, was picked to serve as chief navigator. The fleet set sail on May 20, 1553, carrying with it a letter from King Edward VI addressed to "the Kings, Princes and other Potentates, inhabiting the North-east parts of the world toward the mighty Empire of Cathay."

The ships traveled north along the coast of Norway. But before rounding the North Cape — the very tip of Europe — they ran into a fierce storm. The *Edward Bonaventure*, carrying pilot Chancellor, became separated from Willoughby and the other ships. Willoughby's two ships put in somewhere on the coast of the Kola Peninsula, where he and his men froze to death. Chancellor's ship had better luck. The *Edward Bonaventure* plunged ahead through the icy waters until it reached the White Sea. At the mouth of the Dvina River the ship dropped anchor. Local people told them they were in the land known as Muscovy (Russia). The Englishmen were brought to the court of Czar Ivan the Terrible in Moscow and were lavishly entertained throughout the winter.

In the spring of 1554 Chancellor returned to England, having arranged a trade agreement with the Russian czar. Although a Northeast Passage to Cathay had not been found, the trade pact with Russia proved very profitable. The Muscovy Company, as the Merchant Adventurers became known, sent English cloth to Russia in exchange for furs, timber, and other valuable goods. But even this success did not fully satisfy Sebastian. The dream of reaching Cathay remained uppermost in his mind.

In 1556 Captain Stephen Borough was ordered out with the ship *Searchthrift* in yet another effort to find the Northeast Passage. Although Sebastian was then a white-bearded old man in his early seventies, he was still spry enough to attend a farewell party. As Captain Borough later recalled, "the good old gentleman Master Cabot . . . and his friends banqueted, and made me and them that were in the company good cheer." Caught up in the excitement of the moment, Sebastian "entered into the dance himself among the rest of the young and lusty company."

This is the last we hear of Sebastian. He is believed to have died one year later, in 1557. Like his father, he went to his grave with his dream of reaching Cathay and Cipango unfulfilled. His

Sebastian Cabot.

explorations produced no flourishing colonies, no caravels struggling under the weight of gold, no shortcut to the spices and precious gems of the East. He died without having lived up to his own self-image of greatness.

AFTERMATH

A little over a century after John Cabot's death, the English finally took effective steps to exploit the vast territory opened up by his voyages. In 1606 the Virginia Company of London was formed for the purpose of planting an English colony in the New World. Three shiploads of settlers set out for Virginia the following year. On May 14, 1607, they landed at Jamestown Island and founded the first of the thirteen American colonies.

John Cabot had not failed after all; he had actually succeeded beyond his wildest dreams. When he came ashore on that June morning in the year 1497, he laid the foundation for the future English-speaking countries of North America — Canada and the United States.

A Note on Sources

Much of the information about the voyages of John Cabot comes from several detailed letters written by merchants and diplomats living in London at the time. These primary sources include: the Letter of Raimondo de Soncino to the Duke of Milan, (December 18, 1497), the Letter of Lorenzo Pasqualigo to his brothers in Venice (August 23, 1497), the Letter of John Day to the Lord Grand Admiral of Spain (probably Christopher Columbus) (winter of 1497–98), the Letter of Pedro de Ayala to the Spanish Sovereigns (July 25, 1498). Full text translations of these documents are contained in James A. Williamson, *The Cabot Voyages and Bristol Discovery under Henry VII.* The Letters Patent from King Henry to John Cabot, dated March 5, 1496 and February 3, 1498, still exist in the British archives.

Principal works on the two Cabots are *John and Sebastian Cabot* by Sir Charles Raymond Beazley, *The European Discovery of America* by Samuel E. Morison, and the Williamson book mentioned above.

The Author

Henry Ira Kurtz, a graduate of Columbia University, has also studied at Oxford and the University of Vienna. He is an editor of reference books and has written for *History Today* and *American History Illustrated*, as well as for numerous children's publications and popular magazines.

Index

Age of Exploration, 2-3
Alexandria, Egypt, 8
Arsenal, the, 5
Asia, 1, 8, 10
Astrolabe, 24

Book of Marco Polo, The, 9
Borough, Captain Stephen, 53
Bosworth Field, Battle of, 16
Bristol, England, 12

Cabot, John:
    backed by England, 18-20
    birthdate, 3
    death of, 39-40
    education of, 8-10
    family of, 4
    first voyage, 21-31
        date of departure, 21
        date of return, 31
        food, 23-24
        hardships, 23
        landing site argued, 29
        navigating instruments, 24
    as the "Great Admiral," 35-36
    legacy of, 40-42
    second voyage, 37-40
        clues to wreck of, 39
        date of departure, 37
    as Venetian merchant, 6-8
Cabot, Sebastian, 23
    birthdate, 4
    as chief navigator of Spain, 46
    death of, 53
    false claim to voyages, 2, 43
    first voyage, 45
    as mapmaker, 44
    second voyage, 50
Caboto, Egidius (or Julio), 4
Caboto, Giovanni. *See* Cabot, John
Caboto family, 4
Canada, John Cabot at, 29, 42
Cape Breton Island, possible landing at, 29
Cape Hatteras, Sebastian Cabot near, 45
Cape Race, J. Cabot at, 31
Caravels, 10
Caribbean Sea, 39
Carracks, 10

Cathay, 7, 18, 45
Chancellor, Richard, 52
Charles I, King of Spain, 46, 51
Charts. *See* Mapmaking
China, 5, 7, 9
Cipango, 10, 18
Cogs, 21
Columbus, Christopher, 1, 3, 10, 11, 19
Company of Merchant Adventurers, 52
Constantinople, 8, 11
Cross-staff, 24

Da Gama, Vasco, 42
Dead reckoning, 27
De Medrano, Catalina, 46
De Solís, Juan Diaz, 50

Edward VI, King of England, 52
Edward Bonaventure, the, 53
Elizabeth I, Queen of England, 16
Elyot, Hugh, 14, 23
England, 1, 10, 12
    backing of Cabot's voyages by, 18-20
    claim to New World, 1, 42
    fisheries in New World, 31, 42
    of King Henry VII, 16-18
    relations with Spain, 20, 36
    trade, 14, 53
Ericson, Leif, 29
European trade, 5
Exploration, Age of, 2-3

Ferdinand, King of Spain, 20, 46
Fishing (in the New World), 31, 42
Food, preservation of, 7
France, 10

Greenland, 45

Henry VII, King of England, 16-18, 19-20, 35, 45, 46
Henry VIII, King of England, 46
Hojeda, Alonzo de, 39
Hudson Bay, Sebastian Cabot in, 45

Iceland, 14
India, 5, 42
Indies, the, 5, 50

Instruments, navigating, 24
Isabella, Queen of Spain, 20
Ivan the Terrible, Czar of Russia, 53

Japan, 10

Labrador, possible landing at, 29
La Cosa, Juan de, 39
Letters Patent, 20

Magellan, Ferdinand, 1, 47
Mapmaking, 8, 44, 51
Marco Polo, The Book of, 9
Matthew, the, 21
Mecca, 8
Monarchies, rise of, 10
Muscovy Company, 53

National states, rise of, 10
Navigation, 8, 24-27
    dead reckoning, 27
    instruments, 24
Newfoundland, 29, 31, 37
Northwest Passage, search for, 45, 52-53
Nova Scotia, possible landing at, 29

Ottoman Empire, 11

Pasqualigo, Lorenzo, 35
Polo, Marco, 9-10
Portugal, 11, 18-19, 20, 42

"Queen of the Adriatic," 4-5

Ramusio, Giambattista, 44
Renaissance, 2-3
Richard III, King of England, 16
Russian trade, 53

Searchthrift, the, 53
Ships, 5, 10, 21, 23
    Edward Bonaventure, 53
    Matthew, 21
    Searchthrift, 53

Silk trade, 5
Slave trade, 5
South America, Sebastian Cabot in, 50, 51
Spain, 10, 40, 46-51
    relations with England, 18-19, 20, 36
Spice Islands, 8, 47, 50
Spice trade, 5, 6-8, 11, 42

Taxes, 17
Thorne, Robert, 14, 23
Tordesillas, Treaty of, 20, 36
Trade:
    English, 14, 53
    European, 5
    Russian, 53
    spice, 5, 6-8, 11, 42
    Venetian, 5
Treaty of Tordesillas, 20, 36
Tudor Dynasty, 16
Turkish Empire, 11

Vergil, Polydore, 39
Venice, 4-5
Vikings, 29
Virginia Company of London, 55
Voyages:
    Cabot, John, first voyage, 21-31
        date of departure, 21
        date of return, 31
        food, 23-24
        hardships of, 23
        landing site argued, 29
        navigating instruments, 24
    Cabot, John, second voyage, 37-40
        clues to wreck of, 39
        date of departure, 37
    Cabot, Sebastian:
        false claim to voyages, 2, 43
        first voyage, 45
        second voyage, 50
    Christopher Columbus, 1, 11
    Hojeda, Alonzo de, 39

Willoughby, Sir Hugh, 52